STATE

Atiha Sen Gupta

STATE RED

OBERON BOOKS
LONDON

WWW.OBERONBOOKS.COM

First published in 2014 by Oberon Books Ltd
521 Caledonian Road, London N7 9RH
Tel: +44 (0) 20 7607 3637 / Fax: +44 (0) 20 7607 3629
e-mail: info@oberonbooks.com
www.oberonbooks.com

A catalogue record for this book is available from the British Library.

PB ISBN: 978-1-78319-199-4
E ISBN: 978-1-78319-698-2

Printed, bound and converted
by CPI Group (UK) Ltd, Croydon, CR0 4YY.

State Red was first performed at Hampstead Theatre Downstairs, London on 7 November 2014 with the following cast:

RICHARD	Geoff Leesley
JOYCE	Maxine Finch
MATTHEW	Toby Wharton
LUKE	Samuel Anderson

Writer	Atiha Sen Gupta
Director	Douglas Rintoul
Designer	James Turner
Lighting Designer	Tim Lutkin
Sound Designer	Helen Atkinson

THANK YOU TO:

Rahila Gupta and Guy Slater for reading drafts of *State Red*, giving feedback and helping me to have the confidence to get it from the page to the stage.

Naomi Games for giving me food to eat and food for thought about SC&O19.

Raju Bhatt for your legal expertise.

Will Mortimer for seeing something in *Return*, for your vision and for your great banter.

Edward Hall and Greg Ripley-Duggan for believing in my work and giving it a platform (a very nice platform it is, too).

Douglas Rintoul for taking the pulse of the play, putting it on steroids and surgically removing clunk (this is why I'm not a doctor...). I can't imagine *State Red* without you.

And finally, THANK YOU to my cast Geoff Leesley, Maxine Finch, Toby Wharton and Samuel Anderson if not for getting justice for JJ then for doing justice to my words.

Characters

RICHARD
white, 57 years old (RICHARD wears the uniform
of a high-ranking police officer/smart dressing
gown)

JOYCE
black, 57 years old (JOYCE wears an elegant
green dress/smart dressing gown)

MATTHEW
white, 27 years old (MATTHEW wears a smart
black suit throughout)

LUKE
mixed-race (black/white), 27 years old (LUKE
wears a grey tracksuit and trainers throughout)

SETTING

*The play is set in the open-plan kitchen/living room area of a
large Edwardian house in Muswell Hill, London, UK.*

NOTE ON THE TEXT

*A dash (–) at the end of a line indicates where the following
character should interrupt.*

*The ellipsis (…) indicates where a line or a thought should trail off
and be suspended in the air momentarily.*

'He's not the finest character that ever lived. But he's a human being, and a terrible thing is happening to him. So attention must be paid.'

Linda Loman, *Death of a Salesman* by Arthur Miller.

LIGHTS UP.

LUKE enters through the front door. He heaves a large black shoulder bag into the room. He closes the door behind him.

He stops and stares at everything around him. He walks downstage with the bag and leaves it by the sofa. He stares at it.

He sits on the sofa, checks his watch, exhales and then retrieves a packet of cigarettes and a lighter from his tracksuit bottoms. He lights up.

He gets up and examines a framed photograph on the wall. He squints trying to view a figure in it, as if in disbelief.

A police siren is heard crescendoing, LUKE starts.

He goes to the kitchen, takes one last drag and puts his cigarette out in the sink and throws it into the bin.

He walks up the stairs.

BLACKOUT.

LIGHTS UP.

The front door opens and RICHARD, JOYCE and MATTHEW spill into the room.

RICHARD: *(Acting out opening a champagne bottle, upper-class English accent.)* …Don't shoot that thing at me – I might lose an eye! *(As RICHARD.)* And I'm thinking, hold on – it might actually be an improvement.

MATTHEW laughs, JOYCE smiles.

JOYCE: *(To MATTHEW.)* Don't encourage him.

RICHARD: What? I was miles away! *(Shaking his head.)* Honestly, some people…you'd think they'd be grateful you were just about to pour them a glass of expensive bubbly.

JOYCE: You serving them champagne meant you didn't have to talk to them! *(Indicating MATTHEW.)* If it wasn't for him, I'd have drowned in a sea of titles.

MATTHEW: Anytime, Joyce.

JOYCE: *(Cracking up.)* Did you see her face when I said 'Muswell Hill'?

MATTHEW: Absolute. Legend.

JOYCE: *(As woman, frustrated.)* But where are you really from?

RICHARD: They weren't that bad!

MATTHEW: How would you know? You left us peasants to fend for ourselves!

RICHARD: Hey – whose side are you on?

MATTHEW: *(Standing to attention.)* On the side of truth and justice, sir, like you always taught me.

RICHARD: *(Screwing up his face.)* Forget that bollocks.

JOYCE: Language!

MATTHEW: I'll leave you two lovebirds to it.

JOYCE: Why don't you stay?

MATTHEW: I've got the car.

JOYCE: Just crash upstairs!

MATTHEW: It won't take me a minute.

JOYCE: *(Taking her heels off, wincing and rubbing her feet.)* I don't like you going out late. And you've been drinking.

RICHARD: Why don't you leave the powers of house arrest to me, darling?

MATTHEW: *(Nodding towards RICHARD.)* If anyone stops me, I'll just tell them who I've spent the evening with.

RICHARD: *(Making his way to the stairs.)* Oh – stop – if I had any modesty left, I'd be blushing.

JOYCE: He may run the world, but I run this house – you're staying.

MATTHEW: Thanks for the back-up!

RICHARD: Nothing personal – I've got an extra early start, is all.

JOYCE: *(Beat.)* Why?

RICHARD: Because I have a day job.

JOYCE: And teaching the next generation to be useful members of society isn't?

RICHARD: You know what I mean.

JOYCE: You're up to something.

RICHARD: You're paranoid.

JOYCE: Did the Home Secretary have a word?

RICHARD: Curiosity killed the cat, my dear.

JOYCE: Good job I'm not a cat.

RICHARD: *(RICHARD grabs JOYCE mock violently, she shrieks.)* Miao! *(RICHARD kisses her. To MATTHEW.)* Parental Guidance is advised, lad.

MATTHEW shields his eyes like a child.

JOYCE: I don't know what you're screwing up your eyes for – how do you think you came about?

MATTHEW: *(Pointing at them.)* Not like that. Unless there's something you're not telling me?

RICHARD: No, no. One was enough. *(To MATTHEW.)* You should stay – better to be safe.

A silence.

JOYCE: Who wants a hot drink?

MATTHEW shakes his head, RICHARD nods.

JOYCE makes her way to the kitchen, as she does so she sniffs.

JOYCE: Is that –

MATTHEW: *(Sniffing.)* – Cigarette smoke?

RICHARD: Hey, hey. Don't look at me – I've been clean for seven years.

JOYCE: A cigarette doesn't smoke itself. *(Motioning to MATTHEW.)* And I can't imagine *he'd* allow himself to smoke. You on the other hand –

RICHARD: He sits around all day waiting for something to happen – I'm the workhorse!

MATTHEW: It must be hard keeping the Ivory Tower clean, hey Richard?

RICHARD and MATTHEW exchange silly faces.

JOYCE: Hmmm… *(JOYCE places the kettle under the sink to fill it and sniffs again.)* You little liar!

RICHARD: Not guilty your honour.

JOYCE: Whatever happened to truth and justice?

MATTHEW: Spill the beans.

RICHARD: Honest to god.

JOYCE: You don't believe in god.

RICHARD: What's with all these ad hominem attacks?

MATTHEW: Don't think your northern charm can save you now, you old Sweat.

RICHARD: *(Chuckling.)* Racists – the lot of you! We northerners were the first immigrants, don't you forget… And this old Sweat will be running the city of London soon if you're not careful.

JOYCE: I knew it!

RICHARD: Let's just say…don't be surprised if I'm voted Britain's hunkiest policeman before the year's out.

MATTHEW: *(Laughing.)* Good night.

JOYCE: Help me get some sense out of him.

MATTHEW: *(Shaking his head.)* See you in the morning.

JOYCE: Don't you want a herbal tea, honey?

MATTHEW: How old do I look?

RICHARD: Just don't come crying to us in the middle of the night when you're suffering from the champagne sweats.

MATTHEW: *(Laughing.)* First world problems.

RICHARD: Good night, son.

JOYCE: Sleep well.

RICHARD: *(Examining his uniform.)* I feel like a bloody Christmas tree.

JOYCE: *(Rubbing her eyes.)* You must be glad that's all over.

RICHARD: It's tiring being the best looking couple in the room, isn't it?

JOYCE: You're selling us short – I would have gone for borough! *(Beat.)* I don't know why but everyone kept coming up to me and commenting on how utterly charismatic you are…

RICHARD: *(Grabbing his heart, making a croaking sound, JOYCE is worried.)* You…paying me a compliment? I think I'm having a heart attack.

JOYCE: *(Slapping him.)* Camomile or peppermint?

RICHARD: I'll have the whisky flavour.

JOYCE: Be serious for once.

RICHARD: I'm serious all the bloody time – even more so, now. This is my only space to be a –

JOYCE: Twat?

RICHARD: *(Laughing.)* You do have a way with words, love.

JOYCE: You're not the only Cambridge graduate in the room…

RICHARD: I stand corrected.

RICHARD hugs JOYCE and spins her around so that she is facing the kitchen.

JOYCE: I just wish –

RICHARD: *(Squeezing JOYCE sympathetically.)* I know love.

JOYCE: *(Pause. Smiling.)* When you get this –

RICHARD: If, darling, not when, I don't want to jinx any –

RICHARD sees LUKE. MATTHEW follows behind him.

JOYCE: You happy with camomile then? *(Looking at RICHARD's face, laughing.)* You look like you've seen a ghost!

MATTHEW: Look what I found.

JOYCE turns around and sees LUKE.

JOYCE and RICHARD rush towards him.

JOYCE: Luke? *(Beat.)* Luke!

RICHARD: Hiya kid!

JOYCE: Are you OK?

LUKE: *(After a pause.)* You're all dressed up – you shouldn't have.

JOYCE: Well don't just stand there – come and give your old mum a hug at least.

LUKE steps into JOYCE's embrace – she dots his face with kisses.

RICHARD: Alright – you've had your fill. *(RICHARD hugs LUKE.)* Good to see you, kiddo.

LUKE: Yeah.

JOYCE: When did you get back?

LUKE: Dunno. *(Pause.)* Can't remember.

JOYCE/LUKE: *(At the same time.)* So –

LUKE: Sorry…

JOYCE: No, go on…

LUKE: *(To JOYCE.)* You look beautiful.

RICHARD: *(Clearing his throat.)* Ahem.

LUKE: *(Slapping RICHARD's belly.)* You've put on weight, pops.

RICHARD: This one's a right charmer, isn't he?

JOYCE: *(To LUKE.)* And you've lost it.

LUKE: Where have you been?

MATTHEW: House of Lords. Wish you'd come back earlier – you could have had my ticket.

JOYCE: *(To LUKE.)* Thank *god* you're back.

LUKE: What's with the House of Lords?

MATTHEW: You didn't miss much. Just lots of people trying to impress…lots of people.

LUKE: I called you like, ten times.

MATTHEW: *(Checking his phone.)* Oh shit, sorry, mate.

RICHARD: *We* would have picked you up from the airport…

JOYCE: I could have cooked a special dinner for you. Actually, I have a bit of curry goat left over from lunch?

LUKE: I'm not hungry.

JOYCE: Let me feed you.

LUKE: I want to know how you are.

JOYCE: *(Inspecting LUKE.)* You've lost 12 pounds.

LUKE: *(Impressed.)* How do you do that?

JOYCE: *(Tapping her nose.)* Cup of tea?

LUKE: Not for me, mum. *(Beat.)* Thanks.

JOYCE: I'll leave the teabag in.

LUKE: Seriously, don't worry.

JOYCE: Worry? I'm over the bloody moon. Two sugars or have you cut down? You're a ticking diabetes time bomb waiting to go off, you do know that? *And* it runs through my side – it's just playing with fire to have such a sweet –

LUKE: I don't feel like tea.

RICHARD: You don't look like it either!

JOYCE: Your father's lost none of his sense of humour this past year.

LUKE: *(Smiling.)* That's a shame.

RICHARD: Oi! I was gonna offer you a beer.

LUKE: *(Shaking his head.)* I'm good.

RICHARD: What about some whisky?

JOYCE: *(Giving RICHARD a stern look.)* Richard…

LUKE: You guys have some.

RICHARD: I've got single malt from Edradour – ordered it in especially for you. For when you got back.

LUKE: *(Shaking his head.)* What can I say, I'm a cheap date.

RICHARD: All of this is very suspicious… No tea, no alcohol. *(Eyes widening.)* You haven't become a Mormon have you?

JOYCE laughs.

LUKE: No, of course not.

RICHARD: Just checking. I wouldn't disown you, I'd just think you'd lost the plot.

LUKE: Tea just sets me on edge – don't like the way it makes my heart beat.

JOYCE: Oh, OK, Lukey… You let me know if you want something, though, anything –

LUKE: I'm absolutely knackered.

MATTHEW: Sorry mate – wasn't expecting to find you there.

LUKE: It is my room, dickhead.

JOYCE: *(About to scold, RICHARD shoots her a look.)* Lang –

MATTHEW: And I nearly got into bed with you!

LUKE: Prefer brunettes. Sorry.

MATTHEW sticks his middle finger up at LUKE. LUKE laughs.

MATTHEW: *(To RICHARD and JOYCE.)* I'm telling you this one would sleep through the end of the world!

LUKE: Talking of sleep, you should get some.

JOYCE: We're not leaving you. Not now.

LUKE: I'll be fine. I'm only going from here to my bedroom – how difficult can it be?

JOYCE: I want to hear everything!

RICHARD: Don't argue with your mother – it won't end well.

JOYCE: Are you sure you're alright?

LUKE: Why wouldn't I be?

RICHARD: You did disappear for a year.

JOYCE: Richard!

LUKE: *(To JOYCE.)* It's OK.

MATTHEW: He did email us.

RICHARD: Once!

LUKE: So you wouldn't organise an INTERPOL search team for me.

RICHARD: You make it sound like a bad thing – worrying about our missing son!

JOYCE: *(To RICHARD.)* This is not the time…

LUKE: *(To RICHARD.)* Say what you feel – I respect that.

RICHARD: Someone has to. Look, I'm not having a go. We were just –

LUKE: I know. I'm sorry.

LUKE puts his hand out. RICHARD shakes it and brings him into a hug.

RICHARD: See – I've brought him up well.

JOYCE: You brought him up? *(Kissing her teeth.)* That's the first I heard of it.

RICHARD: *(Conspiratorially winking at LUKE.)* And on that note… *(Ruffling LUKE's hair.)* Your mother's kissing her teeth, it's time to go.

LUKE: Night.

RICHARD spots LUKE's bag.

RICHARD: I'll take your bag up.

LUKE: You don't have to.

RICHARD: I want to. Do something for my boy.

JOYCE: This is your father's idea of child support.

LUKE laughs at the joke.

RICHARD struggles with the weight of the bag.

RICHARD: *(Thoughtlessly.)* What have you got in here, a body?

LUKE's face falls.

RICHARD: It must be all those toiletries you were so fond of. Never did understand why it took you longer to get ready than your own mother. *(Pointing at MATTHEW.)* And that goes for you too. In my day, you had a shit and a shave and called it a night…

RICHARD takes the bag upstairs.

JOYCE: Good to be home? *(LUKE nods.)* I'm happy to stay up with you…?

LUKE: I know where everything is.

JOYCE: Your father doesn't mean… Sometimes he doesn't think.

LUKE: I've heard worse.

JOYCE: If you need anything, and I mean *anything*, just come and wake me up.

JOYCE kisses LUKE three times, on the third kiss –

LUKE: OK mum, we're not in Switzerland…

JOYCE: It's good to have you back.

LUKE: *(Nods, looking around.)* Why are the walls a different colour?

JOYCE: *(Batting the question away.)* I'll tell you in the morning.

JOYCE walks upstairs, frequently looking back at LUKE.

MATTHEW looks expectantly at LUKE: LUKE smiles. They break into their signature handshake which consists of a fist bump, stacking fist potatoes, shaking hands, a finger click, playing a trumpet on their nose and 'pon de river, pon de bank' with their feet.

MATTHEW: Are you going to get some kip?

LUKE: Don't think I'll be able to now.

MATTHEW: Don't feel you need to entertain me. *(Beat.)* I've more than made myself at home here!

LUKE: I can see.

MATTHEW: *(Pause.)* Your mum look pleased to see you.

LUKE: She'd double over like that if the pizza man turned up earlier than expected.

MATTHEW: *(Laughing.)* That's true. *(Beat.)* You look good.

LUKE: Do I?

MATTHEW: *(Laughter tailing off.)* I mean... Not as good as me but...

LUKE: How's the team?

MATTHEW: Marcus?

LUKE: Him, the boys. How are they?

MATTHEW: Yeah, very well.

LUKE: So you're still there?

MATTHEW: Sorry?

LUKE: You've still got a job? You haven't become one of the great unwashed?

MATTHEW: *(Pause.)* Not yet. Fingers crossed, hey.

LUKE: Thanks by the way.

MATTHEW: For what?

LUKE: Being here for my parents.

MATTHEW: Just repaying a massive debt.

LUKE: Do you ever think about him?

MATTHEW: Richard? I think about him all the bloody time
– he's the bane of my –

LUKE: Jerome Johnson.

MATTHEW: Where did you go?

LUKE: *(Pause.)* Just places, you know, here and there. Travelled a bit.

MATTHEW: *(Nodding head.)* Cool. (Beat.) You could have sent me a postcard!

LUKE: Didn't really stay in one place for long, you know how it is.

MATTHEW: I'll let you off then.

LUKE: *(Pause.)* I guess you've been summoned too?

MATTHEW: So you know.

LUKE: It's been a long time coming.

MATTHEW: It's standard procedure. Don't let it stress you.

LUKE: I'm not stressed. I've left stress, shed it like a skin.

MATTHEW: Nothing will come of it.

LUKE: It doesn't matter what the world thinks of you if you're OK with yourself.

MATTHEW: That's the spirit.

LUKE: *(Producing a piece of folded paper.)* My statement…

MATTHEW: They haven't asked for it again have they? They're so incompetent…

LUKE: I want every line in it to be perfect. Maybe you could…read it? Now?

MATTHEW: I've seen it a thousand times before, Luke. It's well written.

LUKE: It's not a short story.

MATTHEW: I'm just saying – it sets out what happened clearly.

LUKE: I wasn't sure what to write –

MATTHEW: There's no need to worry – it's all done now.

LUKE: It's all jumbled up…

MATTHEW: Why don't you sit down?

LUKE: I already know the bad news! *(Pause.)* You remember when we got beat up back in the day?

MATTHEW: We were always getting into scraps.

LUKE: How many times was it deadly serious?

MATTHEW: Hardly.

LUKE: 15 and you were chasing that girl – what was her name?

MATTHEW: Which one?

LUKE: The black girl – there was only ever one black girl – you'd kissed at that under-16s rave where they only served orange squash but we sneaked in Tesco Value vodka. *(Beat.)* Victoria.

MATTHEW: *(Correcting.)* Victory. Her name was Victory. *(Beat.)* She was Nigerian.

LUKE: Victory to the rescue! But someone must have seen you kiss and grind on her like there was no tomorrow. Must admit – you could grind better than any other white boy within a ten-mile radius.

MATTHEW: *(Laughing.)* You taught me everything I know.

LUKE: But the next day the man dem descended. How they even knew where to find us, god only knows… Outside the school gates, not a teacher in sight. They dragged us off: *(Impersonating the boy, barking.)* Which one of you's Matthew? *(As LUKE.)* I didn't say a word – we just looked at each other and kept shtum.

MATTHEW: Thanks.

LUKE: Dude thinking either one of us could be the bastard who's messing with Victory so he gives the nod to both his boys – double the fun – and they beat the living daylights out of us. *(Stressed.)* Out of *you*.

MATTHEW: They beat you up too.

LUKE: Those boys were what, 14, 15? I bet they'd been stopped and searched by police into the double digits by that age – and they took all their frustrations and anger out on you, white boy. You could have been any white boy. *I* might have been Matthew, dry fucking Victory but at least I was one of them – partly one of them. The leader – that dark, handsome boy with the cane rows – he had light grey eyes too – like Jerome. Do you remember?

MATTHEW: I can't imagine I was staring dreamily into the dude's eyes who was beating the shit out of me.

LUKE: Just like Jerome Johnson.

MATTHEW: OK – I get it – they both had grey eyes.

LUKE: Somewhere deep inside me and you – they deposited a seed of hate. We'd messed around before but those were fair fights. We were bloodied and beaten and defeated. Something inside us said, one day there's gonna be payback, don't know how or when but there will be…

MATTHEW: It's all forgiven and forgotten.

LUKE: From that day onwards, we knew what the enemy looked like didn't we? Black boys with grey eyes…

MATTHEW: I didn't get a chance to gaze into his eyes either.

LUKE: His name. You can't say it.

MATTHEW: Johnson. Jerome Johnson.

LUKE: I think about him every day.

MATTHEW: You've got to let it go.

LUKE: I shot a human being dead.

MATTHEW: It's 2am.

LUKE: And?

MATTHEW: He had a gun in his hand.

LUKE: It was a Blackberry!

MATTHEW: We had reason to believe he was armed when we surrounded him.

LUKE: *We* of all people should be able to distinguish between the two.

MATTHEW: It was gleaming in the sun!

LUKE: JJ – those large grey eyes and that dark black skin. Looking at me. With his hands up. *(LUKE puts his hands up.)* He's looking at me like it's K.O. – like he's played one too many video games and wishes he could just step out of this one. We're eyeballing each other. He looks like a little boy who's lost his mum in Marks and Sparks and doesn't know what to do next. And then he mouths it.

MATTHEW: Come on, Lukey, it's past your bedtime.

LUKE: You saw it.

MATTHEW: I was on the opposite side, Luke! I couldn't have seen it even if I'd wanted to.

LUKE: What?

MATTHEW: I was covering him from the back.

LUKE: I thought –

MATTHEW: I wasn't even in the same car as you!

LUKE: *(Beat.)* He mouthed "coconut" and you said "Do it".

MATTHEW: *(Putting his hand on his heart.)* I don't know where you've been or what you've taken but you need help.

LUKE: Coconut. My whole life – distilled into one word. *(Beat.)* I used to see the other black guys working at protests – getting rowdy lefties asking if they felt compromised by being black and a copper at the same time. And their faces are always the same like they didn't even hear the question. They're OK with who they are and what they do but how did Jerome know that I wasn't?

MATTHEW: No one thinks you're a coconut.

LUKE: *(Shouting.)* My mother is black, Matthew! I'm in the police force. I'm a black man shooting other black men for a living.

MATTHEW: You're good at your job.

LUKE: What do you see when you look at me?

MATTHEW: I…I don't see – I see my friend.

LUKE: I don't want to hear that colour blind bullshit, Matthew.

MATTHEW: I see someone I've grown up with, had my first experience of everything with, someone who I can't manage without. And yeah, he happens to be a bit darker than me.

LUKE: I've got a tan…is that what you tell yourself?

MATTHEW: *(Pause.)* OK. Get it out of your system. And tomorrow this will all be forgotten.

LUKE: No one forgets this stuff – trust me I've tried.

MATTHEW: *(Going up to LUKE and holding his shoulders.)* We are friends from day dot and nothing is going to change that, do you understand?

LUKE: *(Crying.)* Because of us a boy is dead. JJ has lost his life!

MATTHEW: Hey – look – don't cry. We were just doing our jobs. It was him or us. We were ordered over the radio to "strike, strike, strike". They called State Red!

LUKE: When Grace and Rodney saw me cry they didn't tell me not to.

MATTHEW: Who are Grace and Rodney?

LUKE: I found them.

MATTHEW: What?

LUKE: 9 months ago.

MATTHEW: By accident.

LUKE: At first they were suspicious. *(Laughing at the memory.)* Actually at first they thought it was a joke. *(Jamaican accent.)* Who is this young bwoy pon the doorstep chatting rubbish? *(As LUKE.)* But when I showed them my ID and told them, really told them who I was, they knew. Then they got angry, upset. But they asked me back. They wanted to know everything about Jerome's last moments. I told them again and again and they'd ask to hear it just one more time. Was he frightened? What were his last words? Was somebody holding his hand when he passed?

MATTHEW: This is not right.

LUKE: *(As if unaware MATTHEW is there now.)* He does look scared, I can't lie Mrs Johnson but once he falls to the floor, we call the paramedics and keep him warm. I seal his sucking chest wound and start compressions. Once the professionals come, I sit next to him and hold his hand and with the other I stroke his forehead. I speak about the weather and he listens – how stupidly British of us – but it is a beautiful day – hot and sunny…

MATTHEW: Luke. Luke! Do you know how serious this is? I don't even know where to begin…

LUKE: His family put a plate of curry goat and rice in front of me – for the policeman that killed their son and said "Eat, eat. Take as much as you like". I cried. Do you know how that feels? Can you understand that?

MATTHEW: You ate with them? Jesus, what else did you do?

LUKE: A family who have lost everything are strong enough to forgive and trust the boy who killed their boy.

MATTHEW: *(Dawning on him.)* You've been in this country all along…

LUKE: Don't tell my mum.

MATTHEW: You didn't travel…at all.

LUKE: I travelled! I travelled from despair to this…here… now. I know you feel it too.

MATTHEW: Feel what?

LUKE: We were put out there – sent to kill by superiors who didn't give a shit – who wouldn't have offered up their own sons.

MATTHEW: We keep the streets clean – we're not soldiers!

LUKE: Tell the truth.

MATTHEW: Excuse me?

LUKE: The Coroner will accept our full accounts – even now! Especially now!

MATTHEW: I gave it. Months ago.

LUKE: I need this inquest, so do you.

MATTHEW: This is too far.

LUKE: If you stand with me, it would change everything. You could get the other boys onside too.

MATTHEW: I think this could be Post Traumatic Stress Disorder.

LUKE: The Johnsons understand the mental and physical pressure we were under.

MATTHEW: People like the Johnsons hate people like us. They hate the police! They'll say and do anything to try and bring us down.

LUKE: All you'd need to do is confirm my account.

MATTHEW: Luke – this is very dangerous.

LUKE: There's nothing dangerous about the truth.

MATTHEW: This isn't it.

LUKE: They forgive you.

MATTHEW: Forgive me for what!

LUKE: I told them – about what you said.

MATTHEW: Take a deep breath, Luke.

LUKE: *(Pause.)* I thought you'd be happy?

MATTHEW: Happy my best friend has made up a story that could drop us in the biggest shit of our lives?

LUKE: But it's the opposite – this will get us out of the shit!

MATTHEW: You've always been too sensitive, Luke. *(No response.)* We'd go clubbing and if you saw a girl...or even a guy...passed out with vomit all over them – you'd sit and clean them up, buy them a bottle of water, call a cab. *(Beat.)* Who does that?

LUKE: I do. You do.

MATTHEW: You know how you used to say I'm always right? *(Beat.)* Well, believe me – I'm saying it now – what happened to Johnson was above board.

LUKE: Matthew, please...

MATTHEW: I understand that there is a certain trauma attached to opening fire and this is why I suggested counselling – right at the beginning. I know a really good guy – I've got his direct line. *(Beat.)* He'll be able to see you first thing tomorrow morning.

LUKE: I don't need a counsellor. *(Beat.)* I needed to see you – I've been going over this on the minute, on the hour, over and over, for a year. It's…like a washing machine that never turns out clean clothes… You're the only one who understands.

MATTHEW: There was no coconut, there was no "do it". This isn't a Nike advert, Luke. There was no time for that – we're talking a matter of split seconds. We pulled a non-compliance stop – and I agree, always have done, that it's not the best way to stop a criminal in his tracks but it's police procedure and it's all we have. We pull the stop and instead of getting out of the car like a normal innocent human being, Johnson starts to do a runner – you only run when you've got something to hide – so we surround him. You on one side – the sun was shining bright in your eyes, do you remember, Lukey? Me? I'm on the other side – I'm watching the back of his head and I've also got my MP5 pointing at him, in case he tries to pull anything funny – so it easily could have been me who fired the shot. Unfortunately for you, he was facing you and had what looked like a gun pointing in your direction and so you shot to save yourself, to save us.

LUKE: It's OK to make mistakes… As long as –

MATTHEW: *(Snapping.)* What has got into you? Why are you so fucking obsessed with Jerome Johnson?

LUKE: You're swearing – you only swear when you're stressed.

MATTHEW: What?

LUKE: Haven't heard you swear all night.

MATTHEW: He's nobody to us! We took a menace to society off the streets. Do you know how many kids watched his example – wanting to emulate him? *(Stabbing his chest.)* We probably saved lives in the long run. We did a good thing, Luke. Why can't you see that?

LUKE: He was just a kid.

MATTHEW: You've got to stop punishing yourself.

LUKE: So few opportunities and then we took away his opportunity to live.

MATTHEW: No more excuses.

LUKE: Granted: JJ was a cocky little shit but who isn't when they're that age?

MATTHEW: Stop.

LUKE: There are people who have done things a million times worse than JJ and we cuff them, try them and throw them in jail. We don't execute them in the streets.

MATTHEW: We didn't have time to have sophisticated philosophy debates – we were on the frontline!

LUKE: I had my Taser, my Glock SLP and my MP5 carbine. So far, so good? Let's count the Taser as one 'bullet', for the Glock there were 17 bullets inside, 17 on my person and 17 in my grab bag, my MP5 had 26 rounds, another 14 on my person and another 66 in my grab bag, you know, just in case. How many's that Matthew?

MATTHEW: I don't know.

LUKE: Well bloody well count! *(Beat.)* 1, 17, 17, 17, 26, 14, 66 makes? *(Beat.)* 158. I had 158 bullets and JJ had none! How is that a fair fight?

MATTHEW: We used reasonable force.

LUKE: Does shooting an unarmed man in the chest sound like reasonable force to you?

MATTHEW: Oh my god. We thought he had a gun.

LUKE: Because he was young and black.

MATTHEW: Because he was a thug. Leave race out of this. Please.

LUKE: You want me to leave race out of this?

MATTHEW: It's what I said. What, you deaf as well as deluded now?

LUKE: Since 1990 1,496 deaths –

MATTHEW: Oh we're not playing this game are we?

LUKE: 1,496 deaths have occurred in police custody: 10 rulings of unlawful killing in inquests – not one single conviction. What does that tell you?

MATTHEW: That the inquest got it wrong, or worse – had it in for us? That if you compare our figures to Brazil's rates of police killings – it pales in comparison, I don't know Luke but those are my initial ideas.

LUKE: 147 of those were black or from an ethnic minority.

MATTHEW: My maths was never as good as yours but that's about 10% which is roughly what you guys make up of the population.

LUKE: You guys? So now we're counting?

MATTHEW: Mate – I didn't mean it like that… You know I didn't mean it.

LUKE: Try telling JJ's parents we didn't fucking mean it!

MATTHEW: I'm just saying those deaths are proportional – it's not like half of deaths in custody were black people – *that* I'd understand.

LUKE: So you're saying the Met isn't racist?

MATTHEW: *(Motioning with his hands.)* You're acting like it's just white people in the Met and black people on the outside!

LUKE: Macpherson found there was institutional racism in our neck of the woods – we've had training on this – black boys laugh when we ask them if they want to join our ranks. Are you really telling me we're not racist?

MATTHEW: *I'm* not racist. I can only speak for myself.

LUKE: Don't say your best friend is black – just don't.

MATTHEW: Come on, man – Bhavna and I dated for years and even considered getting married. I was up for it – she pulled away 'cos her parents wouldn't have liked a white guy in the family. How's that for racism?

LUKE: I don't care where you stick your cock, Matthew! I'm asking you to admit that the Met is institutionally racist.

MATTHEW: *(Shrugging.)* I don't know what you want me to say.

LUKE: When I say the word 'gangster' – first thing that comes into your head?

MATTHEW: Tracksuit, trainers, chains, maybe a cap…

LUKE: And?

MATTHEW: Well we're in London – so they tend to be young black men.

LUKE: There it is!

MATTHEW: I don't believe this!

LUKE: You said it.

MATTHEW: If we worked in Glasgow, they'd be white!

LUKE: When we go looking for gun and knife crime suspects, the first image in our mind's eye is a black man. You don't think that's a problem?

MATTHEW: It's simple demographics, so no.

LUKE: We had dumb intelligence issued by an incompetent police force that thinks any black man under the age of 30 has something to hide!

MATTHEW: Now you're being stupid.

LUKE: You're right, sorry – under the age of 40!

MATTHEW: I wasn't the one who shot him.

LUKE: So now I'm by myself – it was just me, myself and I – wielding that gun? Is that how it's gonna go?

MATTHEW: I'm not saying that. We were a team. But you cannot go around making accusations.

LUKE: You helped me kill him.

MATTHEW: Lying isn't good for your health, Luke. You've already suffered enough.

LUKE: I'm not. Why would I?

MATTHEW: You smoked a lot of weed just after it happened.

LUKE: I'm clean. I haven't touched the stuff since I left. For a whole year.

MATTHEW: Wasn't just weed though, was it? There was alcohol, pills, coke…

LUKE: That was after the incident – not before. I know what happened, I was sober when it happened.

MATTHEW: You were very, very poorly, Luke. Honestly, it broke my heart. Your parents worried about you desperately, so did I.

LUKE: I didn't imagine things.

MATTHEW: And you weren't just content with poisoning yourself, you wanted to poison others – so sick were you with what had happened. I understand.

LUKE: No. *(Pause.)* No.

MATTHEW: Driving on the motorway, in the third lane, drunk, pilled up, coked up, high as a fucking kite. I mean you were really ticking all the boxes and you drove to Marcus' house, didn't you? To shout at him at what, 3, in the morning? You were so worked up that instead of waiting at the front door like a normal human being, you jumped over his gate and smashed his back door in. Marcus initially thought you were an intruder.

LUKE: It was the day after it happened – it was fucked up, I was fucked up – I…I didn't know what I was doing.

MATTHEW: Exactly.

LUKE: You can't compare then and now.

MATTHEW: There are bound to be gaps in your memory.

LUKE: I was high as hell, alright, I accept that.

MATTHEW: You could have killed more people that night.

LUKE: I was trying to… I don't know… Punish him, for what he'd done. Making us go out there on trumped-up barely-there evidence about JJ.

MATTHEW: You can't punish others for *your* actions, Luke!

LUKE: It was a one off.

MATTHEW: Your mum and dad were terrified for you – you know if you'd gone on like that, there was talk of sectioning. It would have killed them but they did discuss it at the time.

LUKE: No… No… Why would they? *I'm* their only son…

MATTHEW: You nearly left them with no option.

LUKE: They said that?

MATTHEW nods.

LUKE: Maybe dad but not mum.

MATTHEW: Your mum was the one pushing for it. For your own protection.

LUKE: Jerome was a victim of the Met and I'm asking that you and I don't go the same way.

MATTHEW: You finished?

LUKE: You don't care at all… Do you?

MATTHEW: I can't believe I was genuinely looking forward to seeing you.

LUKE: We'll only get one opportunity, we speak at this inquest… Or it would be like us killing JJ twice.

MATTHEW: YOU WANT TO TALK ABOUT OPPORTUNITY? *(Pause.)* Johnson wasn't the only one who lacked opportunities in life but some people climb their way out.

LUKE: A boy's died and you're giving me a sob story?

MATTHEW: At school they asked us to do that presentation on our dads, you remember… You rolled into school the next day, smug as shit, wearing Richard's custodian helmet that he'd let you borrow for the day saying *(Impersonating a child.)* My dad gets the bad guys. *(As MATTHEW.)* Ever since that day, I knew what I wanted to be when I grew up.

LUKE: It's not my fault your father walked out on you. We were always an open house for you, still are – you've been sleeping in my bed for the past year like fucking Goldilocks!

MATTHEW: I don't need your charity.

LUKE: So now you've got a problem with our kindness? Fucking hell, Matthew, there's no pleasing some people.

MATTHEW: *(Tearing up.)* You might be black but I've come from nothing.

LUKE: You're crying for your sad little childhood but you couldn't muster a few tears for a dead boy?

MATTHEW: Fuck you I'm not crying.

LUKE: Everyone has their struggle.

MATTHEW: Some more than others.

LUKE: Meaning?

MATTHEW: *I* was the one who grew up in Tottenham, not you.

LUKE: I'm sorry for your hard life, I really am but that's no excuse for what we did.

MATTHEW: I put myself through Hendon, I got noticed, I got myself into the unit. Words like future weren't in my vocabulary. You was –

LUKE: Were. You were.

MATTHEW: *(Shaking his head.)* Forget 'coconut', JJ should have mouthed 'silver spoon'.

LUKE runs towards MATTHEW and they lock foreheads. They become caught in a half-embrace, half-fighting position with each other.

LUKE is about to strike MATTHEW but MATTHEW grabs his wrist.

MATTHEW: You better watch that temper of yours. One life's already been lost.

LUKE lets out a primal sound of frustration/grief, he bends over and starts hyperventilating.

Some moments later hurried footsteps are heard from upstairs.

JOYCE, followed by RICHARD, run down the stairs.

JOYCE rushes to LUKE and rubs his back.

MATTHEW collects his coat.

JOYCE: What are you boys still doing up?

RICHARD: Have you started drinking without me? The cheek!

MATTHEW: *(Chuckling.)* I'm afraid we're just this hyper even without alcohol!

JOYCE: How long's he been like this?

MATTHEW: He'll be OK, you can go back to bed, Joyce.

JOYCE: *(To LUKE.)* Are you alright, sweetie?

MATTHEW: He'll be fine. We were just catching up. Things can get a bit –

RICHARD: Emotional? *(Nodding.)* It's much healthier that way.

LUKE: Depends on the emotion.

JOYCE: I knew we shouldn't have left you.

LUKE: We covered a lot of ground, didn't we, Matthew?

JOYCE: *(To LUKE.)* Why don't you come and lie down on the sofa?

MATTHEW: That, Joyce, sounds like an excellent idea. Good night.

JOYCE: No…no…that wasn't a cue for you to go.

MATTHEW: I've got work tomorrow. *(Looking at his watch.)* Today!

LUKE: *(Straightening up.)* Stay for a drink. You can have a drop. Scotland's finest?

RICHARD: You've changed your tune.

MATTHEW: I'm not one for drink driving.

LUKE: I'll call you a cab.

MATTHEW: There's no need.

LUKE: Dad'll pay for it.

RICHARD: Will I?

MATTHEW: I like my own bed.

RICHARD: Me too – if everyone's OK?

MATTHEW: Hunky dory.

RICHARD: *(To JOYCE.)* See I told you they'd be fine – you worry too much.

RICHARD starts up the stairs.

LUKE: Won't you have a drink with me, dad? Toast my arrival? A shot of whisky. *(Looking at MATTHEW.)* Calm the nerves.

RICHARD: A shot? That sounds like the beginning of a night out. I'm an old man!

MATTHEW: *(Reaching for his coat, to LUKE.)* Take care of yourself.

LUKE: But we've got so much more to catch up on!

MATTHEW: *(Quiet.)* Drop it.

LUKE: Drop what?

MATTHEW: Nothing…

JOYCE: Are you feeling OK, Matthew?

MATTHEW: Nah I'm fine.

MATTHEW goes to the kitchen and pours himself some tap water. He downs it.

RICHARD: *(Chuckling.)* What are you two like? Now we've got two casualties.

MATTHEW: No casualties.

LUKE: Keep your cool.

MATTHEW: My cool is kept. Don't worry about my cool.

> *LUKE retrieves glass tumblers, sets them on the table and fills them up generously with whisky. He picks his glass up and downs it. He offers one to MATTHEW.*

MATTHEW: I said not for me.

RICHARD: My dad always said whisky was the cure for everything: fatigue, wind, heartbreak!

LUKE: Nobody likes a killjoy.

MATTHEW: Good job I don't cave into pressure, then.

JOYCE: What is going on?

MATTHEW: I've got to go.

LUKE: Matthew and I were just discussing JJ weren't we?

JOYCE: *(After a silence.)* We don't need to go into all that now. Rehashing old things.

LUKE: I think we do.

RICHARD: We know the pressure must have been close to unbearable. We understand why you had to get away this past year.

LUKE: Nobody tell me they understand.

RICHARD: We're all on your side here.

LUKE: *(Shaking his head.)* The inquest…

JOYCE: What inquest?

RICHARD: *(Putting his hand up to silence her.)* Not now Joyce.

LUKE: Didn't Matthew mention it?

MATTHEW: Your parents have been busy with other things.

JOYCE: Not that busy.

MATTHEW: It's ages away.

LUKE: I'm going in tomorrow.

JOYCE: But you've already been cleared…

LUKE: By the IPCC? Police investigating police? Give me a break.

RICHARD: Forget those clowns. There's been a thorough internal inquiry. The boy's been cleared by the Met itself.

MATTHEW: *(To RICHARD and JOYCE.)* Luke's been through a big trauma.

LUKE: I'm in the room, you don't need to patronise me – I'm right here.

MATTHEW: It's important to bear in mind.

LUKE: I know the truth. And so do you.

RICHARD: *(To MATTHEW.)* What's he talking about?

MATTHEW: It's obvious that the thought of an inquest has triggered off difficult memories, emotions…

RICHARD: You keep it brief and to the point. You tell them everything you know. And you stay polite. I know it'll be tough but we're right behind you.

JOYCE: You have all our love, Luke, you do know that, don't you?

LUKE: *(Looking at MATTHEW.)* They're not like you, mum.

JOYCE: *They* made you produce many, many statements like they were trying to trip you up. But all of them matched perfectly – you've got nothing to hide.

MATTHEW: That's what I said to him.

LUKE: They matched up because we had our story. We sat in a room all nine of us for nearly as many hours and we plotted what we were going to say. We conferred.

MATTHEW: Yes we sat together but…that's allowed, that's the done thing. In a fatal shooting, we're all traumatised and talking through it actually allows for a clearer picture to emerge.

RICHARD: Is this what got him so worked up just now?

LUKE: Stop making me out to be the hysterical one –
Matthew couldn't even keep his cool a minute ago.

RICHARD: You were having a panic attack, son, it's slightly
different.

JOYCE: We'll support you whatever –

RICHARD: I'll handle this –

LUKE: I won't be giving the cuddly police line, mum, work it
out.

RICHARD: There's no cuddly police line! There's the truth
and then there's that ridiculous gangster family parading
around as civil rights campaigners agitating at every god
given moment.

LUKE: They're not gangsters! They're a loving family.

RICHARD: A loving family doesn't let their son turn out the
way he did.

LUKE: Why can nobody say his name! *(Beat.)* I shot JJ
through the heart.

RICHARD: We know.

LUKE: No. You don't.

MATTHEW: We're all agreed that that's what happened.

LUKE: I…We killed JJ.

RICHARD: We?

MATTHEW: He doesn't know what he's saying –

JOYCE: *(To LUKE.)* Go on…

LUKE: We surround him after he gets out of the car. He
goes to run but we shout: *(Barking.)* "Armed police, Stand
still!" He doesn't move. *(Barking.)* "Hands up, Hands up!"
Matthew's behind me, to my right. JJ turns slowly on his
heel to face me. In his left hand he's got this Blackberry.
Even if it was a gun, we knew he was right-handed so he
couldn't possibly shoot with his left. *(Police-like.)* A 6'2"
black male facing off a 5'10" mixed-race officer. *(As LUKE.)*

38

Jerome stares at me, inspects my face, and mouths...
coconut. Under his breath, I hear Matthew say "do it" –

MATTHEW: For the record can I just reiterate – I was located
opposite Luke – all I could see of Johnson was his back –
the team can vouch for that.

LUKE: "Do it". Quietly, but he says it. I lose my cool, I lose
my nerve, I'm angry. I shoot. I shot.

RICHARD: *(Shaking his head.)* You were all wearing caps, kid.

LUKE: JJ saw enough.

RICHARD: Why would he bother mouthing coconut? He
didn't even know you.

MATTHEW: Exactly.

LUKE: He saw a young black man in police uniform holding
a gun to his head – what else is he gonna think?

JOYCE: Your mind can play tricks on you in a moment like
that. It all coming out now, more than a year later, proves –

LUKE: It wasn't all coming out then because it doesn't look
good, does it?

RICHARD: *(Pause.)* Matthew.

MATTHEW: Yes, sir.

RICHARD: Did you see Johnson mouth anything at any
point during the exchange?

LUKE: Exchange makes it sound like we swapped fire!

RICHARD: *(To LUKE.)* I'm talking now.

MATTHEW: Of course, everything happened over a few
seconds, but as far as I'm aware Johnson did not say or
mouth anything to Luke.

RICHARD: In those seconds, did *you* say anything to Luke?
Or give off any kind of signal to him?

MATTHEW: No, sir.

LUKE: LIAR!

JOYCE: Luke, please.

LUKE: *(To MATTHEW.)* How can you stand there and chat shit?

MATTHEW: In the same way that you can.

RICHARD: *(To LUKE.)* You can be done for perjury if you stand up in court and repeat what you've been saying tonight because none of it's true!

LUKE: *(Shaking his head.)* You just don't get it, do you?

LUKE goes over and pours himself a generous glass of whisky. He drinks from it desperately and bends over semi-retching as it goes down.

RICHARD: You were – are – an upstanding officer, one of the best. *(Beat.)* But I think that being out of work for so long can't have been good for your psyche – you're someone who needs to be active, needs to be helping people.

LUKE: I'm not going back.

RICHARD: Not right away…

LUKE: Not ever.

RICHARD: Is that the whisky talking or my boy?

LUKE: Which boy is that?

RICHARD: You of course.

LUKE: I can't.

JOYCE: We'll take each day as it comes…

MATTHEW: *(Clicking his fingers.)* Marcus would have you back in a heartbeat. After this inquest has cleared you.

RICHARD: I mean obviously you'd have to re-train. Go on a refresher course, as it were. But I think you'd be up to scratch in no time at all.

LUKE: I'm out. I'm done. Not going back to a bunch of murderers and liars!

RICHARD: Keep your voice down.

LUKE: What?

RICHARD: You heard me – there's no need to shout.

LUKE: I'm not shouting.

RICHARD: We're all civilised adults, we can speak calmly to one another.

LUKE: Are you embarrassed by me? Do boys not cry in Manc?

RICHARD: Don't push me.

LUKE: You don't like anyone having another point of view, do you?

RICHARD: Have I ever told you how to live your life?

LUKE: That's because I did everything you wanted me to!

RICHARD: You need to calm down.

LUKE: Until now. Now I'm asking you to have faith in me instead of bullying everyone into silence!

RICHARD: *(Spilling out.)* If I'm asking you to be silent it's because I need to be able to hear myself think about what the fuck I'm going to say to the Home Secretary in three hours time!

LUKE: What?

JOYCE: You got the job.

LUKE: You've already got a job.

MATTHEW: Commissioner.

LUKE: What? When? You didn't say anything.

RICHARD: I don't email people I love – I talk to them – man to man.

JOYCE: Richard –

RICHARD: Please Joyce don't.

MATTHEW: *(Sincere.)* Congratulations.

LUKE: Nothing's changed. If anything, we can use this to our advantage…

MATTHEW: Luke – this isn't *The Bill* – that's not gonna happen.

LUKE: I don't see –

RICHARD: What do you want me to do, then? Just give up my plans to be Met Commissioner? Give up my responsibility to *really* help people?

LUKE: What *I'm* gonna do is going to help people.

RICHARD: I have spent 36 years of my life dedicated to this job, working my way up. Do you know what happened when I married your mother?

LUKE: I don't want to hear this.

RICHARD: If you're so obsessed with the truth, then listen to it!

LUKE: She's black – you married her – what do you want – an OBE?

JOYCE: How dare you?

LUKE: What's your point?

RICHARD: In the force, people weren't really used to seeing mixed marriages… It was alright to have a bit of fun on the side, mess around but you weren't expected to intermarry. Your mother couldn't give a shit and neither could I. Admittedly I didn't progress in the way that I would have liked to. I could sit here and blame racism – or maybe not, maybe it was my own poor performance but I tell you one thing for free: every single colleague of mine got put ahead of me and some of them were shite. *(Beat.)* Now we live in a very different world, a different police force which values diversity, actually seeks it, goes after it. Look at you – you're a fine young officer at the peak of his career and you happen to be mixed-race.

LUKE: Black.

RICHARD: *(Gesturing towards himself.)* And me?

LUKE: You heard.

RICHARD: Alright.

LUKE: So?

RICHARD: So… We paved the way. For people like you to come through and rightly so – you should.

LUKE: This is not about us. This is about something bigger, can't you see that?

RICHARD: What is it about, Luke, apart from you trying to punish me?

LUKE: Why would I want that?

RICHARD: I can see nothing else.

LUKE: Think about it.

RICHARD: Well?

LUKE: Why would I go to inquest and tell a version of events that could lead to me being banged up, if it wasn't true?

RICHARD and JOYCE look at one another, the truth dawning on them.

MATTHEW: In all the truth that he's been spouting, what Luke hasn't said is that in this past year he has met several times with Jerome Johnson's parents – Grace and Rodney.

JOYCE: Is it true?

LUKE: I have met them, yes, so what? It's got nothing to do with anything.

RICHARD: Why have you been hobnobbing with the Johnsons? *(Beat.)* It must have been a bloody coup for them to get you onside.

LUKE: I wanted to pay my respects.

RICHARD: Can't you see how they're using you?

MATTHEW: Luke never left the country. *(JOYCE lets out a gasp.)* He's been meeting up with Grace and Rodney Johnson, having family dinners with them…

LUKE: I happened to be there when they were serving food, once!

RICHARD: *(Shaking his head.)* Exploiting an already vulnerable young man.

JOYCE: You've been here all along?

LUKE: Mum...I just needed to get away.

JOYCE: Get away to *them*? You couldn't talk to me?

RICHARD: Brainwashing.

LUKE: Brainwashing implies they told me something that wasn't true! *(Looking at MATTHEW.)* Both of us know what happened. We're just dealing with it in different ways – he's climbing up the ladder and I'm kicking it away!

RICHARD: I feel bad that I wasn't there for you enough – immediately after it happened. I can't lie, it scared me, I wasn't prepared for it. None of us were.

LUKE: Dad –

RICHARD: My life's work – all for what? Going up in flames because my son's got some bee in his bonnet over a gangster.

LUKE: JJ was not a gangster!

RICHARD: JJ? His name was Jerome Johnson! He's not your brother.

LUKE: He is.

MATTHEW: I can't believe you're choosing their side over us. The people that have trained you, paid you, celebrated you. But most importantly stood by you. Those people want to crucify you – string you up – put you inside for a crime you did not commit –

LUKE: Murder.

RICHARD: Self-defence.

MATTHEW: We neutralised a massive threat.

RICHARD: And you want me to suffer too? Not only will you lose everything, you want me to lose it too? Get real, you stupid boy.

JOYCE: Speak nicely.

RICHARD: The time has gone for speaking nicely Joyce! *(Beat.)* Actually, you wanna speak nicely? You speak to him. You speak to your son.

JOYCE: So now he's *my* son?

LUKE: *(Slamming his glass on the table.)* I've been to JJ's grave 19 times now – once for every year of his life – I gaze down and I try and imagine him there looking back up at me… And I think if we'd had better career advisers and decided to become doctors…or postmen, he might still be alive. I think about each one of his organs dissolving – because of us. I think about how we turned a boy into soil fertiliser. But mostly I think of those eyes – those large grey –

MATTHEW: ARGH ALL THIS HASSLE FOR A SCUMBAG WITH GOLD TEETH!

LUKE: How do you know about that?

MATTHEW: About what?

LUKE: His gold tooth.

MATTHEW: I was there when he was shot.

LUKE: I thought you said you were on the other side?

MATTHEW: *(Beat.)* Yeah, I know. I mean, I was there when he was down, when we converged on him.

LUKE: No. You were keeping the area sterile – cordoning it off.

MATTHEW: I've seen his face in the paper every other week. His family won't shut up about justice for JJ. *(Beat.)* It's in the paper!

LUKE: All the photos of him have been of his mouth shut – I know because his family have been desperate for them to use ones where he's smiling.

MATTHEW: You…you can't have seen them all.

LUKE: How do you know about his gold tooth?

JOYCE: Matthew. Answer the question.

MATTHEW: What? I don't remember stupid details like that. It's like asking me when I realised that Luke had brown eyes.

LUKE: Answer me.

MATTHEW: It's not important.

RICHARD: *(Putting his coat on, to MATTHEW.)* You. Out. Now. *(Beat.)* I'm going to get some fags…

JOYCE: *(To RICHARD.)* So it was you smoking in the kitchen?

LUKE: Actually mum, that was me. Just needed to take the edge off.

RICHARD and MATTHEW leave through the back door.

LUKE pours himself some more whisky and drinks.

JOYCE: Don't you think you've had enough?

LUKE: *(Not looking at JOYCE.)* Is this where you start your good cop/bad cop routine? I'm not falling for it.

JOYCE: If your dad's the good cop, where does that leave me?

LUKE: Did you see that? I can't believe he just walked out with Matthew without saying anything to me…

JOYCE: I hope he'll be having words with him. *(Beat)* I'm so disappointed.

LUKE: Words are not enough mum! A life's at stake!

JOYCE: I understand.

LUKE: Everyone says that but no one really does…

JOYCE: These Johnson people…have they looked after you? *(LUKE nods.)* Do they cook well?

LUKE: *(Pause, smiling.)* Not as well as you.

JOYCE: Now that was the right answer.

LUKE: JJ was an only child.

JOYCE: For a little while after…I thought I might have lost mine.

LUKE: I'd never do anything to hurt you.

JOYCE: Not to hurt me. But you might have hurt yourself – you were a mess.

LUKE: I just couldn't be around all that police chatter – it was deafening.

JOYCE: No apologies, I'm just saying.

LUKE: Mum – I'm just trying to do the right thing.

JOYCE: You're a good boy.

LUKE: I'm telling the truth.

JOYCE: I believe you.

LUKE: Why didn't you say anything?

JOYCE: How could I? Ever since this job's been dangled in front of Richard he's become hard to reach.

LUKE: You have to support me on this. Stand up to him. To them.

JOYCE: You'll never win. Your father is just too determined.

LUKE: The truth is powerful.

JOYCE: No one will believe you with the history you have, the drinking, the drugs, your sudden disappearance of a year. It's not just the Johnsons with fancy lawyers. The Met's legal team are the best game in town. They will bury you with every little mistake you've ever made…

LUKE: I'll be a good witness. I know how to present myself. I already know the suit I'll wear. I'll say "yes sir" and "no sir".

JOYCE: So you go to inquest…

LUKE: OK.

JOYCE: Then what?

LUKE: I'll say what happened.

JOYCE: That there was no gun? That you killed the wrong boy? That there was a cover up?

LUKE: It would be stronger if Matthew backed me but I don't need him. My testimony will blow the jury out of the water. They'll have no option but to return a verdict of unlawful killing.

JOYCE: What then?

LUKE: Then a criminal case might be brought against me and Matthew by the CPS.

JOYCE: What happens?

LUKE: I don't know, mum, I haven't got a crystal ball with me.

JOYCE: Worst case scenario?

LUKE: Worst or best, depending on how you look at it… We get sentenced. Matthew – less – as he didn't pull the actual trigger. I get a reduced sentence for having been honest and submitting a full account at inquest.

JOYCE: How many years are we looking at?

LUKE: I'm no legal expert.

JOYCE: Substantial?

LUKE: Maybe.

JOYCE: Do you know what they do to police officers on the inside?

LUKE: I'll be different. I'm a cop that did right by JJ.

JOYCE: Don't be naive. An officer is an officer. Tarnished forever. They'll have a field day with you.

LUKE: You're getting carried away thinking about all of this. It might never happen.

JOYCE: OK, so let's say you do time. You finish your sentence, maybe early release for good behaviour, you come out. And?

LUKE: I'll look for a job. I'll start again.

JOYCE: All your degrees'll come in handy, then.

LUKE: Do you think I would have joined the Met if it wasn't for dad and Matthew? They practically twisted my arm.

JOYCE: Twisted arm or not, you've spent 8 years in the force! It's all you know.

LUKE: *(Beat.)* I'll be able to look myself in the mirror.

JOYCE: You're going to inquest to look yourself in the mirror?

LUKE: You know what I mean.

JOYCE: Do you think you'll be on speaking terms with your father?

LUKE: I'm his son.

JOYCE: That's not an answer.

LUKE: You'll talk him round.

JOYCE: What happens to his job?

LUKE shrugs.

JOYCE: There is no way in hell your father will be able to accept the Commissioner post. Even forgetting anything so fancy, he'll be talked out of his current job too.

LUKE: They can't fire him for something I did.

JOYCE: Wake up Luke! This is life: they won't fire him but they'll call him in for a little "chat" and all parties will decide that it's for the best that he moves on. And even if he is brave enough to fight it, they will make his working life a living nightmare.

LUKE: You think it's an easy decision for me to lose my freedom, my reputation?

JOYCE: Of course not. But you have to realise your decisions have consequences not only for you but for all of us – most of all your father!

LUKE: I'm prepared for that.

JOYCE: That's not your decision to make!

LUKE: *(Putting his hands to his head.)* I can't believe this…

JOYCE: Believe it.

LUKE: Why are you sticking up for them?

JOYCE: I'm on your side, Luke. Why can't you see that?

LUKE: I need more than sweet words, mum.

JOYCE: And did you even think about what would happen to me?

LUKE: No one can touch you – you're removed from it all.

JOYCE: For nearly 40 years I have been at every single do of your father's: advised him, smiled at crowds, shaken hands, kissed babies. *(Beat.)* There's no denying it, my blackness has helped him. People in the so-called "community" see him and then they see me and they think – that copper, he's alright. He's kind of one of us. But if you speak up in that court, I'll lose everything. *(Pause.)* We still have a mortgage on this house – your father won't have any money coming in…

LUKE shrugs.

JOYCE: That's it? You're shrugging? I'm being serious.

LUKE: *(Smiling.)* You wanna know what I find serious? The fact that a boy is dead because of me and all you can think about is your mortgage.

JOYCE: You're twisting my words.

LUKE: That's the saddest part – I'm not.

JOYCE: You're young, Luke. You don't know how things operate.

LUKE: This past year, I have gone through more shit than most people do their whole lives.

JOYCE: On top of everyone losing their jobs, and all of our friends deciding not to invite us around anymore, do you know what else will happen?

LUKE: Enlighten me.

JOYCE: When you testify, the press will be all over it. I can see the headlines now: MIXED-RACE POLICE FAMILY IN INQUEST HELL – TOP COPPER BETRAYED BY OWN SON.

LUKE: I'll be anonymous.

JOYCE: What?

LUKE: I'll have a codename – a letter and two numbers.

JOYCE: *(Pause.)* You've really done your homework, haven't you?

LUKE: No one will be able to link me to him.

JOYCE: If your father becomes Commissioner, he will not be able to so much as burp without it being tweeted across the world – they will find out.

LUKE: How do you think Grace and Rodney feel?

JOYCE: I'm talking about *us*!

LUKE: And I'm talking about *them*! Every other week, there's an article smearing their son. Ever since it happened, the media has gone to town on them. They're worried the inquest itself will go against them because of all the false reporting. Don't you understand how the machine works, mum? The police not only killed JJ, they've got the media to assassinate his character.

JOYCE: I don't run the media! I'm just one woman.

LUKE: You're one woman whose support would make all the difference.

JOYCE: I'm nobody Luke.

LUKE: How do you sleep at night?

JOYCE: Temazepam. Lots of it.

LUKE: I'm being serious.

JOYCE: So am I.

LUKE: It's almost like you don't want the Johnsons to get justice. How would you feel if it was me?

JOYCE: Touch wood. Don't talk like that.

LUKE: You didn't grow up a million miles away from Dawn – imagine – for one minute that your son was shot dead by the police. What would you do?

JOYCE: OK. Two parents in Tottenham will be happy you grass up the police but for how long? How long will it take

for the buzz to wear off to the fact that they will never see
their only child again?

LUKE: That is very cynical and unfair.

JOYCE: Life's unfair – where did you get the notion that it
wasn't?

LUKE: And you're arguing to make it even worse!

JOYCE: You will do more damage than good. Your father has
worked so hard –

LUKE: I don't want to hear you paying homage to a man
who'll probably take Matthew's side…

JOYCE: Unlike any of his colleagues, he has actively pushed
to improve race relations in this borough, in London,
across the UK. He was the first to push for race equality
training, he turned up, took notes, asked questions. It
wasn't tokenistic. He genuinely cares about black people
in this country, in the force or outside. If you allow him to
accept the post he will fight for them…for us.

LUKE: What's your point?

JOYCE: He's a good man, Luke.

Beat.

JOYCE: Who else is being considered for Met Commissioner?

LUKE: How would I know? *(Beat.)* They're not my problem.

JOYCE: They should be.

LUKE: Just some pompous police folk probably.

JOYCE: Those pompous police folk will be running the city of
London if you get your way.

LUKE: What?

JOYCE: Seven people on the shortlist, how many of them give
a damn about black people, equality, social justice?

LUKE: I haven't met them, I wouldn't like to say.

JOYCE: I have. None of them care about anything apart from
their own careers and maybe their families.

LUKE: That doesn't change the fact of JJ.

JOYCE: There would be no JJ if your father was around! JJ would be walking the streets now if your dad was in power.

LUKE: Yeah?

JOYCE: Of course! Imagine JJ going about his business, taking his parents out, I don't know, for an expensive dinner somewhere nice – Italian! Imagine him falling in love for the first time, how good that would feel. Going to college, maybe even university. Imagine JJ walking on air because life was going alright for him.

LUKE: No...he's gone.

JOYCE: Future JJs. The JJs of tomorrow – they'll be safer with your father in charge. He'll overhaul the whole system. He's been banging the drum against Stop and Search for decades! Before you were born! He's always hated the way it unfairly targets young black men. *(Beat.)* For one thing, he'll never send boys like you and Matthew out on such little evidence. *(Beat.)* And when he does send the units out, they'll be properly equipped...with cameras so any and every shooting will have footage in real time – no cover ups, no lies.

LUKE: You really think he'd make a difference?

JOYCE: I *know* he would. Your father was shouting from the rooftops about Stephen Lawrence at a time when all the Met wanted was for everyone to be quiet and batten down the hatches. Your father refused to compromise his principles. *(Beat.)* You were only little but he'd put you to bed on the weekends and come to me, troubled, and say Luke so easily could be Stephen in a couple of years – something's got to be done about it.

LUKE: You didn't tell me that before.

JOYCE: I'm telling you now.

LUKE: OK.

JOYCE: You asked me why the walls were a different colour from when you were here last? The day you left, he was devastated. He didn't cry but he got in the car, drove to B&Q and came back with a ridiculous amount of paint that we didn't need and started to strip the walls, sand them, repaint them. He spent weeks on it, getting it just right – there's not a drop where it shouldn't be. *(Pointing to a wall.)* This, Luke, is the colour of his grief.

LUKE stares at JOYCE, taking it all in.

JOYCE: Is my boy hungry now? How can you say no to my curry goat and rice?

LUKE: I am a bit peckish, yeah.

JOYCE: Of course you are. A mother can tell these things.

JOYCE runs over to the kitchen. She takes out a bowl and a fork and fills it with rice and curry from the two pans on the stove. She heats it up in the microwave. She rushes back to LUKE and hands it to him. He takes it and attempts to appear self-contained but the moment he smells it he gobbles the food up quickly, messily. JOYCE stands over him and strokes his forehead.

JOYCE: Is it nice?

LUKE: *(With food in his mouth.)* Delicious.

JOYCE: There's plenty more where that came from.

LUKE: Thanks, mum.

JOYCE: I've had plenty of practice. If you stay right here, mum's going to put some meat on those skinny bones of yours in no time at all.

LUKE: *(Finishing his last mouthful.)* Yeah.

JOYCE: *(Taking the bowl.)* Let me get that. You want some more?

LUKE: Maybe a bit later.

JOYCE: We're a good team.

LUKE: You and me?

JOYCE: You, me, dad. People have always commented on us looking like the perfect family: they'd say what a beautiful unit, you're all so interesting, so vibrant. *(Beat.)* I've always been proud of…us.

RICHARD and MATTHEW enter.

RICHARD: *(Sniffing.)* Nice curry goat?

LUKE: The best.

RICHARD: Is it spicy enough for me?

LUKE: You might have to add some hot sauce.

RICHARD: Nice chat with mum?

LUKE: Always have nice chats.

RICHARD: Good, good. Maybe we should all knock off for the night. Talk in the morning.

LUKE: *(Pause.)* I'm sticking to my statement. *(Beat.)* From before.

RICHARD: Oh… That's wonderful.

MATTHEW: It's the right decision, mate.

LUKE: Yeah.

RICHARD: Your mum could always talk you round.

LUKE: She's got the gift of the gab.

RICHARD: Nothing wrong with that – runs in the family.

LUKE: I need to sleep.

RICHARD: *(Blocking LUKE's way.)* What? No!

JOYCE: *(To RICHARD.)* Let him past.

RICHARD: *We've* got more celebrations to get through than the chocolate box. *(To LUKE.)* You were the one who wanted to have a drink – I'm ready for you now.

LUKE: Another time.

MATTHEW: We cool?

LUKE: I guess.

MATTHEW puts a closed fist towards LUKE to start their handshake. LUKE looks at MATTHEW and does nothing.

MATTHEW: Don't leave me hanging…

LUKE reluctantly fist bumps MATTHEW but does not do the whole handshake.

MATTHEW: I'm glad we're all friends again. I'll leave you to some well-earned family time. *(Beat, to RICHARD.)* Good luck tomorrow. And whatever you do – don't press the snooze button!

RICHARD: Thanks.

MATTHEW: See you Joyce.

JOYCE: *(Without looking at MATTHEW.)* Bye.

MATTHEW looks at LUKE sadly and leaves through the front door.

RICHARD pours whisky into three glasses and hands them round.

RICHARD: A toast! To us! To changing the world!

They raise their glasses and take a sip.

JOYCE: *(Screwing her face.)* I don't know what you boys see in this stuff.

RICHARD: *(To LUKE.)* Remember how we'd sit by the fire, drinking whisky and putting the world to rights?

LUKE: I missed that.

RICHARD: Don't be silly… There's nothing to miss. We can do it all the time from now on. Tell me a day. Go on.

LUKE: *(Shrugging.)* Tomorrow?

RICHARD: Tomorrow it is. *(Grabbing the whisky bottle.)* You, me and our good friend here.

JOYCE: I thought for a minute you were talking about me but oh no…

RICHARD: *(Laughing, embracing JOYCE.)* Come here, you. *(Embracing LUKE with his other arm.)* And don't think you can escape either. Just goes to show, you're never too old for a group hug.

JOYCE: GO TEAM US!

LUKE: *(Smiling.)* Mum – never say that again…

They release themselves from the group hug and take another sip in comfortable silence.

RICHARD: …And once I'm Commissioner, they won't be able to touch you.

LUKE: What?

RICHARD: You just need to go back to them – probably best to call actually and just explain that everything you'd said was due to your depression. Just say that you're sorry for their loss and for wasting their time.

LUKE: Who's 'them'?

RICHARD: The Johnsons –

LUKE: I didn't confide in them because I was mentally ill…

RICHARD: You're getting the wrong end of the stick, kid.

LUKE: I don't think I am.

RICHARD: I'm just saying… Now that you're 100% behind me, our only threat is external – it's coming from them.

LUKE: You still think of them as 'they'? As 'them and us'. *(Beat.)* You always have.

RICHARD: Don't take it so seriously –

LUKE: Dad – I am 'they', I'm 'them'.

RICHARD: You're not, son. You're mine. You're ours. You're polite and well-spoken and you give up your seat to old people on the bus.

LUKE: Mum said that when I was small and Stephen Lawrence died, you would worry about me. She said that you saw me in him and feared for the future. Well here it is, dad. The future's arrived and it could be me next. I look close enough to JJ. If I'm out of work clothes, walking down the street, if I get in the wrong car, make the wrong friend, get the wrong officer on my case then I could be a goner too. If you saw me in Stephen why can't you see me in JJ?

RICHARD: Apples and oranges, Luke.

LUKE: They were both boys who shouldn't have been killed.

RICHARD: Jerome Johnson was no Stephen Lawrence. Johnson was a violent, threatening, gangster who dabbled in hard drugs. Stephen was a bright young man with his whole future ahead of him. He never hurt a fly.

LUKE: So what are we saying? What are you saying? We can kill black men who act up but not those who want to become architects?

RICHARD: Get real Luke. JJ didn't just "act up". He was a criminal.

LUKE: He had no criminal record!

RICHARD: He was about to. If you hadn't intervened.

LUKE: This is not *Minority Report*! You can't punish people before they've done something wrong!

RICHARD: No one wanted anyone to die. You didn't wake up that morning and think "I'm going to kill somebody today and I'm going to enjoy it", did you?

LUKE: Put it this way – what if JJ was a white man? A young, ambitious, white man with clean blonde hair, bright blue eyes and a crisp suit. What then?

RICHARD: *(Shaking his head.)* He wasn't.

LUKE: Humour me. Let's say he was tall and handsome and well-educated and spoke like the people on Radio 4. Let's imagine we hear stuff here and there, it becomes enough to start to gather intelligence on him, we mount an operation, we follow him in unmarked cars, and then we pull a hard stop – you with me? *(No response.)* ARE YOU WITH ME RICHARD? *(RICHARD nods reluctantly.)* And then, let's say dude gets out the car – in a parallel universe, this handsome white boy called Jerome Johnson – gets out and runs, he runs as fast as his skinny little legs can carry him. What do we do? *(Staring at RICHARD.)* Do we stand and shoot or do we take one look at him and think, fuck, we've really cocked this one up?

RICHARD: Do you know the hoops I've had to jump through since you've been away? I feel like a racehorse that everyone's riding. I was the Met's favourite but the only stain on my record was you, do you know that?

LUKE: Likewise.

RICHARD: We carry out thousands of operations a year and very rarely the unspeakable happens. But look at the level of scrutiny we put ourselves through.

LUKE: *(Pointing at RICHARD's feet.)* If you call this scrutiny, I'd hate to see what corruption looks like.

RICHARD: We have the most moral police force in the world, Luke!

LUKE: You're so wrapped up with them, you can't even see yourself anymore, dad! It breaks my heart to look at you. I used to think you were the best human being I'd ever met. This past year, I'd think about your catchphrase "truth and justice" and just repeat it to myself. I held it close, it comforted me. *(Pause.)* If you became commissioner, you'd only change the cherry on the top. You'd end up being just like all the rest of them. And I don't blame you – the system would swallow you whole. *(Beat.)* It already has.

RICHARD: *(Checking his watch.)* I don't have long.

LUKE: *(Quiet, wounded.)* Seeing as JJ was their only child, when he was small, from ages 0 to 10, his dad who still fancies himself as a bit of a photographer decided to take a photograph of his boy every single day. Can you imagine? That's like over 3,000 images of this one little kid. Once Grace and Rodney had decided to trust me, they got all of these albums out and I went through every single photo – studying each one like it was for an exam. I somehow felt like I was resurrecting JJ by opening up these pages, asking questions like where was this one taken and who's that? My favourite one is of JJ as a 7 year old – he was 2,685 days old when this picture was shot. It's a bright sunny day – blindingly sunny, like the day he died. He's standing in the park, half in–half out of his mother's arms. JJ's got this massive smile on his face and his body's twisted back. Grace said that just as Rodney was taking the photo, she decided to tickle her boy – he was ticklish under his left armpit – where I shot him. Anyway he twisted back and smiled and that moment was captured forever. *(Beat.)* In that picture he looks like death could never, ever touch him. I look at that photo and I wonder if my bullet tickled on its way out. I look at that little boy and I wish I could reach into that photograph, grab him and tell him to never grow up – to stay exactly how he is: young, safe, ticklish.

RICHARD: That would be the right thing…

LUKE: *(Pained.)* And you're asking me not to tell the truth? *(Silence.)* Well…?

LUKE and RICHARD stare hard at each other.

LIGHTS FADE TO BLACK.

End of play.

BY THE SAME AUTHOR

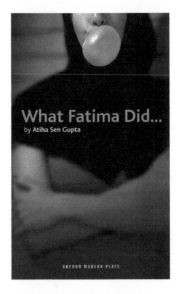

What Fatima Did...
9781840029765

Fatima Merchant is feisty and strong-willed. At 17, she drinks, smokes and parties. On the eve of her 18th birthday, without word or warning or explanation, she adopts the hijab. Suddenly, to her friends and family she is no longer the Fatima they thought they knew.

What Fatima Did... is a funny and provocative exploration of attitudes to identity, freedom and multiculturalism in contemporary London.

WWW.OBERONBOOKS.COM

 Follow us on www.twitter.com/@oberonbooks
& www.facebook.com/OberonBooksLondon